# EPIC FLIGHTS

David Jefferis

Illustrated by
Ron Jobson
and Michael Roffe

**Franklin Watts**
London   New York   Toronto   Sydney

First published in 1987 by
Franklin Watts
12a Golden Square
London W1R 4BA

First published in the USA
by Franklin Watts Inc.
387 Park Avenue South
New York, N.Y. 10016

First published in Australia
by Franklin Watts
Australia
14 Mars Road
Lane Cove, NSW 2066

UK ISBN: 0 86313 521 8
US ISBN: 0 531 105075
Library of Congress
Catalog Card No: 87 50780

**Technical consultant**
Tim Callaway, RAF Museum,
Hendon, London

**Maps drawn by**
Sunrise Studios

**Designed and produced by**
Sunrise Books

© 1987 Franklin Watts

Printed in Belgium

# EPIC FLIGHTS

## Contents

# Introduction

The 1920s and 1930s were among the most exciting and adventurous years in the history of flight.

They were times of trailblazing flights across the world. Pilots risked their lives, often flying in unreliable machines, to be first to cross the Atlantic Ocean or to reach the other side of the world.

An air trip we take for granted today, such as the flight from America to Europe over the North Atlantic, is a comfortable experience. Passengers are often more interested in the in-flight movie than concerned with the stormy ocean below.

The same trip was long and dangerous for pioneer aviators. Charles Lindbergh had to stay awake for 33 hours on his solo transatlantic flight.

Apart from takeoff and landing, today's airliners fly in the smooth air of the upper atmosphere. Pioneer planes couldn't fly very high, so pilots and passengers flew at the mercy of gales, fog, storms or other bad weather along their flightpath.

Single-seat cockpit

Wooden propeller

Single engine

Wood and fabric construction

De Havilland Gypsy Moth

Amy Johnson

4

# Long-distance flyers

The two airplanes below are typical of the machines used on record-breaking flights in the years between World War I and World War II.

The aircraft also represent old and new technologies. On the left is a biplane De Havilland Gypsy Moth. It looks little different from the fighters of World War I and was made of similar materials. A framework, made mostly of wood, was covered with stretched, painted fabric – a construction known as "stick and string." This particular aircraft, *Jason*, was flown by a famous British pilot, Amy Johnson.

The other aircraft is a Ford Tri-motor. The Ford was a monoplane, and its metal construction, multiple engines and enclosed cabin are all features of today's aircraft. The Tri-motor shown here, the *Floyd Bennett*, was the first plane to be flown over the South Pole. It was part of an Antarctic expedition led by the American explorer, Richard Byrd, in 1929. He is shown here dressed in the thick furs that were essential in the sub-zero temperatures of the polar regions.

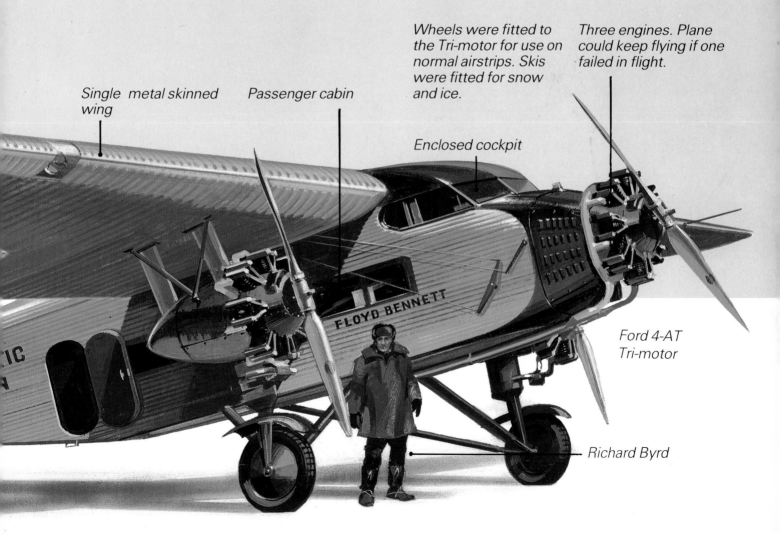

*Wheels were fitted to the Tri-motor for use on normal airstrips. Skis were fitted for snow and ice.*

*Three engines. Plane could keep flying if one failed in flight.*

*Single metal skinned wing*

*Passenger cabin*

*Enclosed cockpit*

FLOYD BENNETT

*Ford 4-AT Tri-motor*

*Richard Byrd*

# Across the Atlantic

As World War I ended, in November 1918, the demands of wartime aviation were replaced by the challenges of peacetime adventure. These included long-distance flights across the world.

A converted Vickers Vimy, a British bomber, was chosen for the first non-stop transatlantic flight. In place of bombs it carried fuel. The pilot was John Alcock, the navigator Arthur Whitten-Brown. They started from Newfoundland, flying east, because the winds normally blow in that direction, making their task a little easier.

At 4.12 pm on June 14, 1919, Alcock taxied the heavily loaded Vimy across the bumpy ground of Lester's Field, near St. John's in Newfoundland. The

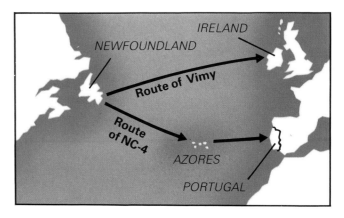

△ Alcock and Brown made the first non-stop transatlantic flight.

Read's team of three flying boats stopped at the Azores.

plane lumbered into the air, just clearing treetops as it slowly gained height. The first hours of the flight were no problem, but soon fog closed in. The rest of the journey was often flown in cloud or through atrocious weather. The first incident was a split exhaust pipe on the right-hand engine – a lick of flame roared out of the open exhaust for the rest of the flight.

Later, Alcock nearly crashed the plane. In mid-cloud he lost his bearings, and the plane fell downward in a confusing spiral. The Vimy broke out of cloud 30 m (100 ft) above the ocean, and Alcock pulled the plane out of its dive with 15 m (50 ft) to spare.

Alcock and Brown flew on with no radio to report on progress as the power generator had failed early in the flight. After sunrise the next morning they were flying through heavy snow. The fuel overflow gauge was covered in snow and unreadable. Whitten-Brown climbed out of the cockpit to clear it. In

△ An American flying boat was the first plane across the Atlantic. With Lieutenant Commander Albert Read in charge, the NC-4 arrived in Portugal eleven days after leaving Newfoundland. Read landed in Lisbon on May 27, 1919. The NC-4 was the only one of the three planes to finish the journey.

his own words, "the gauge was fixed on one of the center section struts. The only way to reach it was by climbing out of the cockpit and kneeling on top of the fuselage, while holding a strut for the maintenance of balance. This I did, and the change from the sheltered warmth of the cockpit to the biting, icy cold outside was startlingly unpleasant." Alcock had to climb out several times before the weather improved.

At 8.15 am on June 15, Alcock

*△ Just after sunrise, Alcock lost control of the Vimy in thick cloud. He managed to pull the plane out of a spiral dive just above the waves, narrowly avoiding disaster.*

spotted two tiny islands – land! Ten minutes later the flyers crossed the coast of Ireland. They found a clear area for landing – but it turned out to be a bog. As Alcock landed the Vimy, it nosed over into the soft ground. But no one was hurt and the Atlantic had been conquered by the two flyers.

# Flying the mails

Carrying the mail was an important part of flying in the 1920s. Letters took a long time to go long distances. Someone sending a letter from Paris to South America could not expect a reply before six to eight weeks had passed.

Aircraft were capable of speeding up the process. Even so, if a mail plane flew into bad weather or strong head winds, it could be overtaken by a fast train down on the ground. But over long distances, aircraft held out great promise. After their Atlantic flight, Alcock and Brown handed over a small bag of mail, which they had carried on the plane as a symbol of things to come.

Charles Lindbergh, later famous as a transatlantic flyer, flew the mails in the United States for several years. Among the planes he flew were ex-US Army machines, bought from salvage sales. The military two-seaters carried mail in the front cockpit, where the army pilot used to sit. Lindbergh flew from the rear, in what had been the observer's seat. One foggy night he had to abandon such a plane. Lost and out of fuel, he jumped overboard and parachuted to the ground. He was uninjured and immediately went to search for the wreckage of his plane, which had crashed nearby. He recovered the mailbags from the front cockpit and took them straight to the nearest post office to be put on a train!

▽ Mail flying could be dangerous if the weather was bad or the plane had engine trouble. In September 1926 Charles Lindbergh had to bail out of his mail plane when he ran out of fuel and thick fog made landing impossible.

# Getting to the destination

Aircraft today are watched on radar screens and directed by flight controllers. Every airliner carries its own highly accurate navigation equipment and weather radar. In the 1920s and 1930s, radar and accurate weather forecasting did not exist. Once an aircraft took off, its crew was on its own. Radio was a help but often unreliable. Navigators depended on clear skies, careful observation and a little luck.

## Contact navigation

*This is flying point-to-point, reading the ground below like a moving map. It is fine while skies are clear, but no good in cloudy weather. In 1921, the British plowed a furrow 800 km (500 miles) across Iraq for their pilots to follow!*

## Dead reckoning

*This allows for a plane drifting off course. If there is a crosswind, then a pilot has to head slightly into the wind to avoid being blown sideways. On long flights, the slightest error can result in a plane being far off-course.*

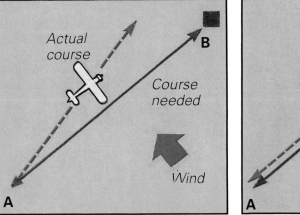

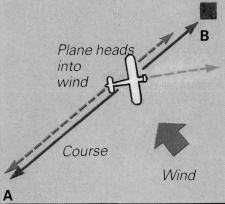

## Star fixes

*In clear skies a navigator can use a sextant to check the heading of a plane against a known point, such a Polaris, the Pole Star. The plane shown here is a German Dornier Wal ("Whale"), a flying boat used on many long-distance flights.*

# Race to the North Pole

The North Pole was a magnet for explorers and as soon as reliable planes were available, aviators tried to fly there. In fact, an air expedition was not a new idea. In 1897, three Swedish balloonists tried a 30-day drift over the

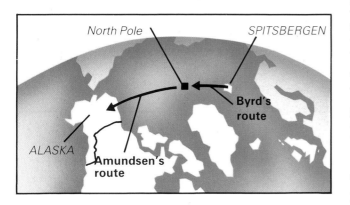

△ Byrd and Bennett made a return trip to the Pole and back from Spitsbergen. Amundsen's airship went on to Alaska.

Pole. Sadly, they had to abandon the balloon after three days and died out on the ice. Two frozen bodies were found years later. The third is still lost.

By May 1926 two air teams were on Spitsbergen island, racing to be the first flyers over the Pole. Norwegian explorer Roald Amundsen was with an Italian team, using a big airship, the *Norge*. In charge of an American team was Richard Byrd. He planned to use an aircraft – a three-engined Fokker F.VII/3m – for the Pole attempt.

The two teams were competing, but on friendly terms, and Amundsen's men helped the Americans when they hit trouble with the Fokker.

On May 9, 1926, Byrd and his pilot, Floyd Bennett, took off while the

airship team was waiting for good weather. After eight hours flying Byrd and Bennett reached the Pole. They circled the area while Byrd double-checked their position (there is no particular landmark on the ice to show exactly where the North Pole is). Then they flew back to base at Spitsbergen. The return trip took 15 hours 28 minutes and covered a distance of 2,575 km (1,600 miles).

Amundsen's team was ready two days later. The airship flew over the Pole and continued on to land in Alaska. An American had made the first trip to the North Pole by land (Peary in 1909) and now Americans were first to reach it by air. Amundsen became the first man to reach both the South Pole (in December 1911) and the North Pole. In 1929 Byrd flew a Ford Tri-motor over the South Pole.

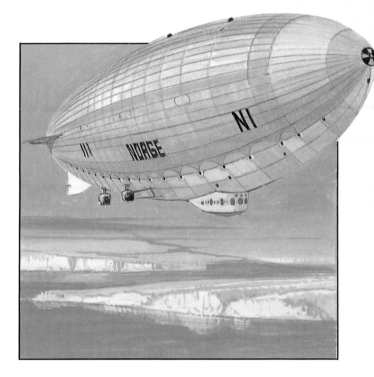

▽ Byrd's Fokker lifted off the bumpy snow at 1.02 am – in summer there are 24 hours of daylight at the Pole. Apart from an engine oil leak there were no problems during the long flight.

△ The Norge was an Italian-built airship, with Umberto Nobile in command. Norge was 106 m (348 ft) long. Slung underneath the huge craft were a control car and three engine pods.

# The lone flyer

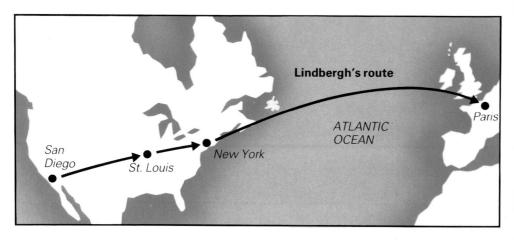

**Lindbergh's route**

San Diego — St. Louis — New York — ATLANTIC OCEAN — Paris

Charles Lindbergh was an airmail pilot who planned a very daring venture – a solo flight from New York to Paris.

In 1927, with money from businessmen in St. Louis, he ordered a single-seat monoplane from Ryan Airlines of San Diego. It was a version of an existing design, the Ryan M2, but by the time Lindbergh had finished modifying it the *Spirit of St. Louis* was pretty nearly a brand new aircraft.

To test his plane, Lindbergh flew from San Diego to New York, stopping at St. Louis to show it to his sponsors. On May 12, 1927, he landed at Curtiss Field, Long Island, to prepare for the long overwater trip. Richard Byrd, the polar explorer, offered Lindbergh the use of his own Roosevelt Field, which had a longer takeoff runway. The *Spirit of St Louis* was towed by a truck to the new airstrip.

A week after arriving on Long Island, with good weather forecast, Lindbergh was ready. The *Spirit of St Louis* was loaded with fuel, a life raft, five sandwiches and a canteen of water,

△ Lindbergh's flight took him from San Diego to New York, then on to Europe.

▷ Lindbergh covered a distance of 5,810 km (3,610 miles). After landing at Le Bourget, shown on the right, he was mobbed by enthusiastic crowds. Thousands of people broke through police barriers to welcome the American flyer.

but no radio. Lindbergh climbed aboard, the engine was started and at 7.52 am on May 20 he opened the throttle and the plane roared off the muddy, rain-sodden runway.

Haze, cloud and ice forming on the wings were problems, but the biggest problem of all was staying awake. Through the long first night Lindbergh saw shapes and visions in the moonlit cloudscapes around him – volcanoes, towers, bottomless pits. After 16 hours he had covered 2,400 km (1,500 miles) – halfway to Ireland! Two hours later

came the first trace of dawn, and with it Lindbergh lost command of his eyelids. They shut, and he lifted them with his fingers. They shut again, tight as glue. In the 20th hour he dozed off.

The plane went into a diving roll – and he jerked awake to recover control. The flight continued like this, with Lindbergh fighting the urge to sleep.

After 27 hours in the air, he saw some fishing boats and circled low overhead but mysteriously, no one came on deck. So he flew on, sure that land couldn't be far ahead. An hour later he spotted the rocky coast of Ireland. From then on all thought of sleep left him, as he flew low over fields and villages.

He passed over Ireland, southern England and, finally, France. As darkness fell for the second time he followed beacons leading to Paris. He circled the Eiffel Tower and landed to a hero's welcome at Le Bourget airport at 10.24 pm on May 21. The trip had taken 33 hours 39 minutes.

# Southern Cross

△ In Fiji Smithy narrowly avoided disaster when the Southern Cross nearly ran into some trees.

▽ The route covered 11,265 km (7,000 miles). The Southern Cross is now displayed at Brisbane Airport.

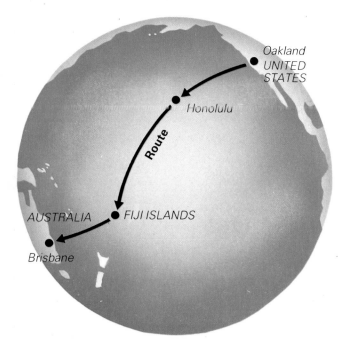

**S**ome daring flights had proved it was possible to fly the Atlantic, but people still thought the Pacific Ocean was too wide to cross by air.

In 1928 an Australian, Charles Kingsford Smith, proved them wrong. "Smithy" wanted to start an airline and a record-breaking flight was a good way to attract financial backing. Smithy and his partner, Charles Ulm, raised money in the United States to buy a plane. Two Americans joined them for the flight, James Warner as radio operator and Harry Lyon as navigator.

On May 31, 1928, the four airmen boarded their plane, the *Southern Cross*, and took off from Oakland, California, heading out over the ocean. The flight took them all the way across the Pacific, stopping at Honolulu and

the Fiji Islands. The only landing area on Fiji was a park – and it wasn't quite big enough. A last moment swerve avoided some trees and the *Southern Cross* stopped in a cloud of dust. Luckily the plane only had light damage.

On June 10 they landed at Brisbane, Australia. They were heroes, and money came flooding in for future flights. Kingsford Smith and Ulm started an airline, Australian National Airlines. This was not a success, however, as the loss of an airliner in mountain country forced its closure. Charles Kingsford Smith continued breaking records until 1933, when he disappeared off Burma. Four years later a wheel of his aircraft was found floating in the sea.

## More epic flights

The late 1920s were great years for aviators. Long distance flying records were regularly broken, though not all flights ended in success.

Undercarriage was abandoned after takeoff

Two Frenchmen made a brave attempt to fly from Paris to New York in 1927. Charles Nungesser, a World War I fighter ace, flew with Francois Coli in a Levasseur PL-8. They crossed the Irish coast on May 8, but were lost somewhere in the Atlantic.

The first east–west Atlantic flight was made in 1928. The three-man plane was a German Junkers W-33L. The single engined aircraft was flown from Ireland, and crash-landed on the snowy Labrador coast of Canada on April 13.

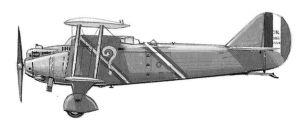

Three years after Nungesser and Coli's brave attempt, a French plane made a non-stop flight from Paris to New York. Dieudonne Costes and Maurice Bellonte flew their brightly coloured Breguet XIX to New York, landing on September 2, 1930.

# The "Line"

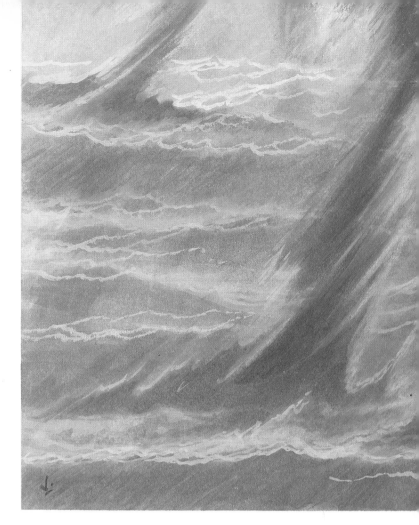

**E**ven before the end of World War I French aircraft maker Pierre Latécoère was thinking of the challenges of peacetime aviation. In 1919 he founded an airline, Lignes Aeriennes Latécoère, often known simply as "The Line." The aim was to open postal flights to South America. At that time anyone mailing a letter in Paris had to wait about two months for a reply. Latécoère thought that an air service could cut this to a week.

By 1928 the Line was established down the coast of Africa and in South America. The next step was to link the two continents by an "air bridge" across the South Atlantic. Senegal to Brazil was the shortest crossing.

On May 12, 1930, the Line's best pilot, Jean Mermoz, taxied a Latécoère 28 floatplane out from the loading dock at St. Louis in Senegal. He opened the throttle, and with a roar from the single Hispano-Suiza engine the plane lifted smoothly off the water. The flight had several spectacular moments. At one point, the three men aboard flew out of cloud to see dark coiling tentacles, snaking from the sea to the clouds above. They were waterspouts, and in the moonlit night they looked a fantastic sight. Mermoz steered the floatplane between the waterspouts to land safely at Natal on the coast of Brazil.

In the 21 hour flight, Mermoz had turned Pierre Latécoère's airmail idea into a real service – the plane's load included 130 kg (285 lb) of mail.

△ Jean Mermoz flew between the water spouts safely. He went on to complete 23 Atlantic flights, an impressive record at the time.

▽ The mail route followed the coast of Africa, skirting the Sahara Desert. Then it crossed the ocean, before going to South American cities.

**Dangers of the post flights**

The Line's flyers had to contend with many dangers. Pilots forced down in the Sahara desert could die of thirst or starve before they were found. If hostile Arab tribesmen came across a pilot, he could be tortured or killed. If the captured pilot was lucky, the Arabs might let him live in order to sell him back to France for a ransom.

In South America there were dangers too. Winds in Patagonia could reach 160 km/h (100 mph) or more. One Line pilot, flying over the Andes mountains, crashed in a blizzard. Believing he was beyond hope of rescue, he trudged through the snow, with no survival rations, for a week before finding people to help him.

# Faster and faster

◁ Deperdussin won the first Schneider Trophy race in 1913.

▷ Curtiss R3C-2 won the 1925 race at 374.28 km/h (232.57 mph).

Many of the technical advances of the 1920s and 1930s were in engine reliability and fuel economy. Both were needed by aviators flying vast distances over land and sea. Metal construction made aircraft stronger and easier to make. Speed was the other vital factor, and the fastest planes of the time were the seaplanes competing for the Schneider Trophy.

The first race was held in Monaco in 1913, and a French Deperdussin won, at a speed of 73.63 km/h (45.75 mph). At the ninth contest in 1926, the record speed was raised to 396.7 km/h (246.5 mph), by an Italian Macchi. Then Britain won three contests in a row and the rules said they could keep the cup if that happened. The winning Supermarine S6B blasted past the line at 547.305 km/h (340.08 mph). But the last, 1931, "race" was really no race at all as the British were the only competitors! The United States did not

enter, and neither France nor Italy had planes ready to fly.

The Italians, however, later went on to fly their new Macchi MC 72. The plane had a pair of engines, one behind the other, each driving a propeller rotating in opposite directions. This cured a problem of some racing planes.

The tremendous power of a racer's engine created a powerful turning force, or torque, as the throttle was opened. This tended to make one float dig into the water and more than one seaplane ended up plowing around in a circle on the water, unable to build up speed for takeoff. The MC 72's two propellers cancelled out the torque effects, making takeoffs easy. In 1934 Francesco Agello flew the MC 72 at a record 709.209 km/h (440.68 mph).

Agello's seaplane record lasted for 29 years until a Russian Beriev Be-10 flying boat broke it in 1961.

▽ Macchi MC 72 set a world speed record for seaplanes in 1932 and another in 1934.

◁ Supermarine S 6B gave Britain the Schneider Trophy in 1931. The plane's design led to the famous Spitfire fighter of World War II.

## Dressing for flight

Standard flying outfit

High-altitude outfit for Everest expedition

Heated goggles

Oxygen mask

Fur lined leather jacket

Fur lined gloves and boots

Parachute

Flight clothes were made mostly for warmth. Open cockpits were chilly, and even enclosed cabins could be cold and drafty at great heights.

To keep warm, aviators wore helmets, goggles and fur lined gloves, jackets and boots. High altitudes led to extra problems. There is not enough life-giving oxygen much above 3,050 m (10,000 ft). The result of oxygen starvation is anoxia, which can lead to a pilot passing out, with death not far behind. The first flights above Mount Everest, in 1933, used experimental oxygen equipment.

# Over Mount Everest

Mount Everest is the highest mountain in the world, and in the 1930s no one had yet climbed it. In 1933 the British mounted an expedition to fly over the 8,848 m (29,028 ft) peak. The Everest team used two Westland biplanes for the dangerous attempt.

The most important survival gear was oxygen equipment, essential for high altitudes. Heated oxygen cylinders were racked in the aircraft, with pipes joining them to the oxygen masks of the crews. Heated goggles were used because, in the icy cold, eyeballs would freeze if unprotected.

By April 1933 the expedition was based in northern India, preparing for the flight to Everest, about 270 km (170 miles) away. On the morning of April 3 they were ready. Four men, two per plane, put on their heated flying suits and oxygen equipment. They tested all the connections, as any electrical fault or oxygen failure could be fatal. All was well, and at 8.25 am, the two planes took off into a shimmering heat haze.

They flew up out of the haze until, at 5,791 m (19,000 ft) they emerged into cold, vividly clear air. Everest and the surrounding mountains, still 70 km (50 miles) away, glittered white and sparkling in the bright sunshine.

Then Clydesdale, the pilot of the lead plane, had trouble with his oxygen supply. His eyesight blurred and he had violent cramps in his feet. He turned on the emergency oxygen, and after some deep breaths recovered enough to keep

flying. He kept the oxygen on full for the rest of the flight. Colonel Blacker, leader of the expedition, sat behind Clydesdale, working the cameras. As they neared Everest, the plane was caught in a vicious downdraft, and was blown down towards the peaks below. The other plane was in an even worse state – but an icy upcurrent helped both aircraft. At the last moment they climbed out of danger.

**M**eanwhile Bonnet, the cameraman in the second plane, stepped on his oxygen pipe, fracturing it. He tied a handkerchief around the crack, and tried to take more pictures, but collapsed. His pilot turned to see him pass out and decided to fly over the summit, take some pictures, then spiral

△ In the lead plane were Clydesdale and Blacker. Following them were McIntyre and Bonnet.

▷ Mount Everest is considered the highest peak. Some scientists now think K2 may be higher.

down quickly to give Bonnet a chance to recover.

Just before 10.00 am, Clydesdale flew through the snow plume blowing off the mountain. Five minutes later the plane cleared the menacing chisel of the summit.

Bonnet survived the trip, though he was an unhealthy dark green color as he came to.

# Race to Australia

On October 20, 1934, a crowd of 60,000 people elbowed to watch 20 planes lined up on the grass at Mildenhall in England. With a crackling roar the two engines of the first plane, a small red Comet racer, burst into life. It howled into the air, to be followed by the other planes. The stream of aircraft headed east; their target, Melbourne in Australia, was over 18,000 km (11,000 miles) away. This was the start of the MacRobertson Race, the longest air race ever.

The race was divided into speed and handicap sections and any number of crew could be carried. This resulted in a wide range of competing aircraft, from single-engined types to airliners. The De Havilland Comet was a small two-seater, specially built for the race. The design had several novel features such as a retracting undercarriage and very thin wings to help the little plane cut through the air smoothly. The makers guaranteed a top speed of 322 km/h (200 mph) although its engines were not especially powerful.

Three Comets started, but the first retired with mechanical trouble after reaching Pakistan in record time. The second Comet, flown by Charles Scott and Tom Campbell Black, landed in northern Australia with engine trouble. A telephone call to the engine's designer helped them guess that the "problem" might be just a faulty oil pressure gauge. They gambled that the engine was going to run – and won the bet. They flew on to win the race. The flight took 70 hours 59 minutes.

The Comet's win was impressive, but the aircraft had been specially designed for the race. What few people expected was the runner up. In second place, less than 20 hours after the Comet arrived, came a Douglas DC-2 airliner. Aboard were two crew members, three passengers and bags of mail. The Douglas could have arrived even sooner, but it got bogged down in mud on landing in northern Australia. Flying in third came another airliner, a Boeing 247D.

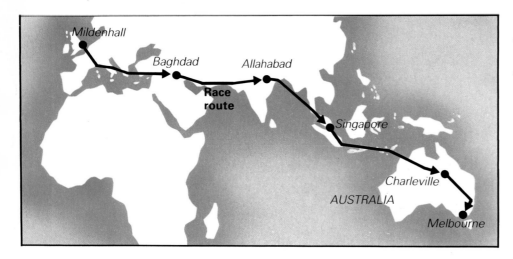

◁ The MacRobertson air race course covered 18,186 km (11,300 miles), completed in five sections.

▽ The winners of the race were very clean designs. From the DC-2, Douglas developed the DC-3, the most successful transport plane of all time. Boeing's 247 was an advanced design too. The Comet formed the basis of the World War II Mosquito light bomber. The winning Comet was stored in pieces for many years. In 1985 volunteers started restoring the plane. It is now in flying condition again, for air show displays.

# The pilot who disappeared

Amelia Earhart was the most famous woman flyer of the 1920s and 1930s. In 1928 she flew across the Atlantic with Lou Gordon and Wilmer Stultz. Only men had made the flight before, and as the first woman to do so she became famous as soon as the trip was over. She went on to complete many epic flights including a solo Atlantic trip in 1932 and the first solo flight from Hawaii to California in 1935.

She had one flying ambition left, to fly around the world, and in 1937 she took off from Oakland, California, to fly eastward on a world trip. The flight went well across South America, Africa and India. By July 1, 1937, she and her navigator, Fred Noonan, had reached New Guinea. There, they had to wait for a raging storm to stop before they could fly on. By the next morning the skies had cleared, and they took off on the long haul to Howland Island, 4,200 km (2,610 miles) away. Over such a long distance navigation had to be completely accurate – the slightest

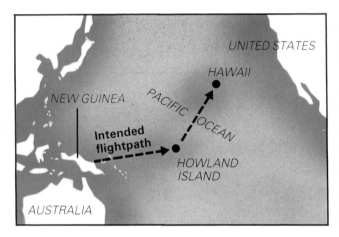

UNITED STATES

HAWAII

NEW GUINEA

PACIFIC OCEAN

**Intended flightpath**

HOWLAND ISLAND

AUSTRALIA

△ Earhart's last flight went east around the world. It ended during the hop across the Pacific from New Guinea to Howland.

▽ Before taking off from New Guinea in their Lockheed Electra, Earhart and Noonan had to wait out a fierce tropical storm.

error meant that the flyers would be lost over the Pacific Ocean.

The American ship *Itasca*, based at Howland, received a garbled radio message early the next morning. The radio operator heard "cloudy . . . visibility bad." Other faint calls were heard, including "we should be overhead but we don't see you. Fuel almost exhausted." A last message came in at 8.45 am ". . . we are turning round . . ." No one heard any more and despite a 16 day search by eight ships of the US Navy, nothing was found of the two flyers or their aircraft.

There were lots of theories about their disappearance, including one that they had landed on a Japanese held island and were shot as American spies. But there was no proof of anything other than a tragic navigation error.

**Amy and *Jason***

*Amy Johnson, like Amelia Earhart, was a trailblazing woman pilot. In 1930 she flew solo from England to Australia, the first woman to do so. The flight took 19 days to complete. Jason was the small biplane in which she made the trip. It was a De Havilland Gypsy Moth, a more powerful version of the Moth, a* *plane which was cheap to buy and easy to fly. You could tow one behind your car, fold its wings and park it in your garage. The idea was to make flying very popular.*

*In fact, owning an aircraft has never become as easy or as cheap as having a car, but light aviation is now an important part of the world of flying.*

# The longest flight

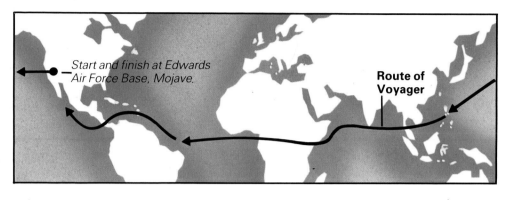

Start and finish at Edwards Air Force Base, Mojave.

Route of Voyager

◁ *Voyager flew west around the world. Rutan and Yeager couldn't avoid some heavy storms on the flight. The trip covered a total of 40,252 km (25,012 miles).*

The golden age of epic flights was in the 1920s and 1930s. But in the 1980s there was still one great flight to make – around the world, non-stop and unrefueled.

*Voyager* was the odd-looking aircraft in which Dick Rutan and Jeanna Yeager made the flight. The plane had long, thin wings and twin booms on either side of the fuselage. Almost all of the structure was filled with fuel tanks. The roar from the rear engine was enough to cause permanent hearing damage in three hours. Rutan and Yeager flew with experimental headsets to protect their ears. They took food and water, pre-packed in separate containers.

Takeoff was from Edwards Air Force Base in the Mojave desert on December 14, 1986. The wings were so full of fuel that they drooped down to the ground. As *Voyager* slowly gained speed down the runway, both wingtips scraped along the tarmac. Rutan, in the pilot's seat, couldn't see this as the booms were in the way. But the ground crew could, and many expected a fireball if a spark ignited the fuel. But all was well, and *Voyager* lifted into the sky, though it used most of the runway.

It was an uncomfortable flight. The wings flexed up and down, and in doing so heaved the fuselage up and down too, like a boat on waves. "You don't get airsick – you get seasick," said Rutan. During the flight they steered clear of the worst weather, guided by mission control back at Edwards. Using satellite pictures to check storm positions, the volunteer controllers talked to *Voyager* by radio. Even so, Rutan and Yeager flew into vicious storms over Africa.

Much of their time was spent pumping fuel among the 17 tanks, to keep the plane in balance as fuel was burned up, and calculating whether there was enough to get home.

## First around the world

*The first world flight was in 1924. On April 6 four Douglas World Cruisers left the USA, flying east. One plane crashed in Alaska, another sank after landing in the Atlantic. The remaining two Cruisers arrived back on the American continent on September 28.*

*The first solo world flight was made by Wiley Post in July 1933. He returned to New York seven days, 18 hours, 49 minutes after takeoff. He flew in a streamlined Lockheed Vega monoplane, named the Winnie Mae.*

▽ Only the rear engine stayed on during Voyager's 187 km/h (116 mph) cruise. The front engine gave extra power for takeoff and climb. The crew shared a tiny cabin about the size of a telephone booth. They crawled around each other to take turns at piloting the plane. When full of fuel the wings drooped downward, then flexed up in flight.

Voyager landed on December 23, with just 69 litres (18 gallons) of fuel left in the tanks.

# Air data

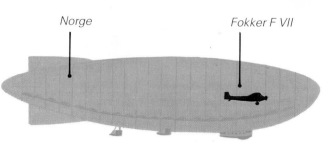

Norge          Fokker F VII

*Norge airship compared in size with a Fokker F VII.*

**H**ere are the most important aircraft described in this book, shown to scale. The PL-8, W-33L and Breguet XIX shown on page 15 are also to the same scale. The aircraft range from small single-seaters to big airliners.

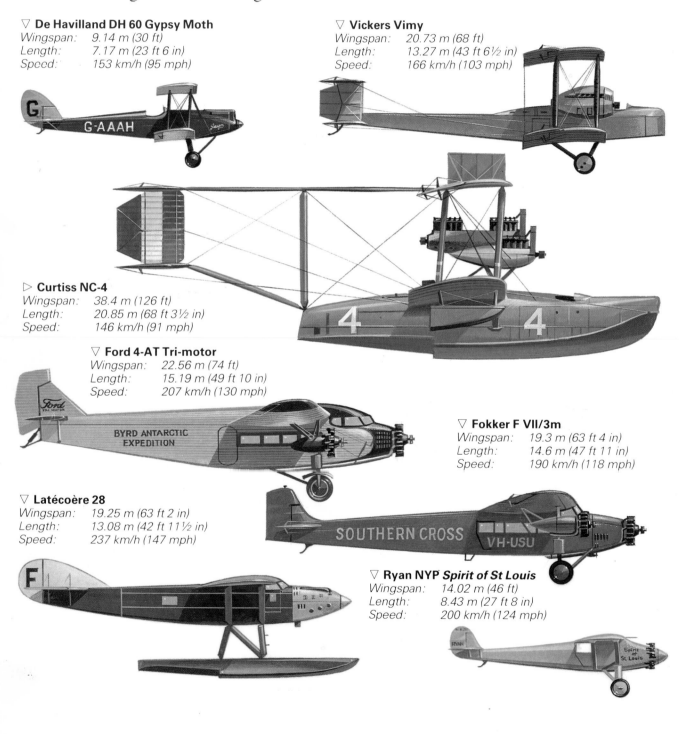

▽ **De Havilland DH 60 Gypsy Moth**
*Wingspan:* 9.14 m (30 ft)
*Length:* 7.17 m (23 ft 6 in)
*Speed:* 153 km/h (95 mph)

▽ **Vickers Vimy**
*Wingspan:* 20.73 m (68 ft)
*Length:* 13.27 m (43 ft 6½ in)
*Speed:* 166 km/h (103 mph)

▷ **Curtiss NC-4**
*Wingspan:* 38.4 m (126 ft)
*Length:* 20.85 m (68 ft 3½ in)
*Speed:* 146 km/h (91 mph)

▽ **Ford 4-AT Tri-motor**
*Wingspan:* 22.56 m (74 ft)
*Length:* 15.19 m (49 ft 10 in)
*Speed:* 207 km/h (130 mph)

▽ **Fokker F VII/3m**
*Wingspan:* 19.3 m (63 ft 4 in)
*Length:* 14.6 m (47 ft 11 in)
*Speed:* 190 km/h (118 mph)

▽ **Latécoère 28**
*Wingspan:* 19.25 m (63 ft 2 in)
*Length:* 13.08 m (42 ft 11½ in)
*Speed:* 237 km/h (147 mph)

▽ **Ryan NYP** *Spirit of St Louis*
*Wingspan:* 14.02 m (46 ft)
*Length:* 8.43 m (27 ft 8 in)
*Speed:* 200 km/h (124 mph)

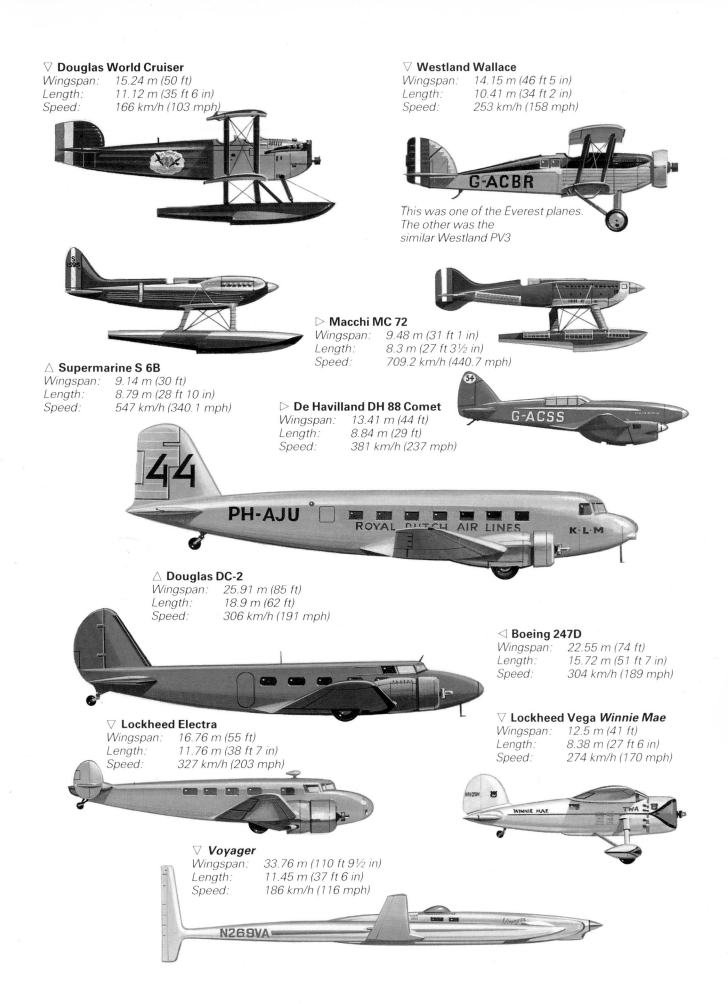

▽ **Douglas World Cruiser**
*Wingspan:* 15.24 m (50 ft)
*Length:* 11.12 m (35 ft 6 in)
*Speed:* 166 km/h (103 mph)

▽ **Westland Wallace**
*Wingspan:* 14.15 m (46 ft 5 in)
*Length:* 10.41 m (34 ft 2 in)
*Speed:* 253 km/h (158 mph)

This was one of the Everest planes.
The other was the
similar Westland PV3

▷ **Macchi MC 72**
*Wingspan:* 9.48 m (31 ft 1 in)
*Length:* 8.3 m (27 ft 3½ in)
*Speed:* 709.2 km/h (440.7 mph)

△ **Supermarine S 6B**
*Wingspan:* 9.14 m (30 ft)
*Length:* 8.79 m (28 ft 10 in)
*Speed:* 547 km/h (340.1 mph)

▷ **De Havilland DH 88 Comet**
*Wingspan:* 13.41 m (44 ft)
*Length:* 8.84 m (29 ft)
*Speed:* 381 km/h (237 mph)

△ **Douglas DC-2**
*Wingspan:* 25.91 m (85 ft)
*Length:* 18.9 m (62 ft)
*Speed:* 306 km/h (191 mph)

◁ **Boeing 247D**
*Wingspan:* 22.55 m (74 ft)
*Length:* 15.72 m (51 ft 7 in)
*Speed:* 304 km/h (189 mph)

▽ **Lockheed Electra**
*Wingspan:* 16.76 m (55 ft)
*Length:* 11.76 m (38 ft 7 in)
*Speed:* 327 km/h (203 mph)

▽ **Lockheed Vega** *Winnie Mae*
*Wingspan:* 12.5 m (41 ft)
*Length:* 8.38 m (27 ft 6 in)
*Speed:* 274 km/h (170 mph)

▽ *Voyager*
*Wingspan:* 33.76 m (110 ft 9½ in)
*Length:* 11.45 m (37 ft 6 in)
*Speed:* 186 km/h (116 mph)

# Inside the cockpit

Here you see the inside of Lindbergh's *Spirit of St. Louis*. He had no direct forward view. Instead, a periscope poked out of the left side, the view being displayed on a mirror in the instrument panel. He didn't worry too much about having poor forward view as there was no air traffic over the Atlantic, and he could peer out of the side windows and through the periscope when it was time to come in for landing.

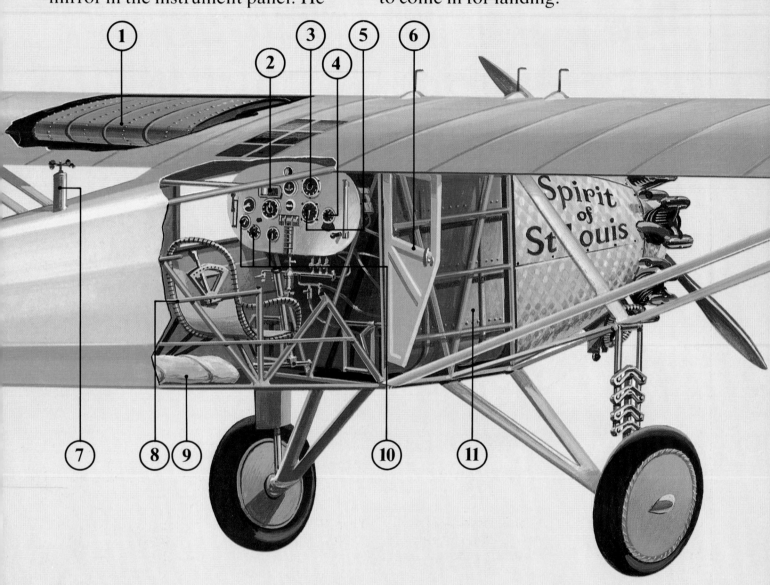

1 Fuel tanks inside the wings.
2 Periscope mirror. The periscope itself pokes out of the left fuselage side.
3 Altimeter gives height reading.
4 Clock.
5 Air speed indicator.
6 Cabin door.
7 Compass equipment.
8 Wicker seat, with engine throttle on the left cockpit side, hidden in this view.
9 Liferaft.
10 From left, these three gauges show oil and fuel pressure and oil temperature.
11 Main fuel tank fills fuselage in front of cockpit.

# Glossary

**Airship**
Lighter-than-air balloon, lifted by the buoyancy of a gas such as hydrogen. Airships have motors for propulsion. Modern airships use helium as a lifting gas since it cannot catch fire, like hydrogen.

**Air speed indicator**
Instrument that shows a plane's speed through the air. A small open tube pointing in the direction of flight measures the pressure of wind against the plane, converting this into the speed, displayed on an indicator. It is not a measure of ground speed – a tail wind, for example, will make an aircraft fly faster.

**Altimeter**
Instrument used to measure height. It is basically a barometer to measure air pressure, which falls with height.

**Anoxia**
Condition caused by lack of oxygen, a danger with all high altitude flights. Symptoms included failing eyesight, followed by loss of consciousness. Death is certain unless oxygen can be supplied quickly.

**Biplane**
Aircraft with two sets of wings, one above the other. A monoplane has a single set of wings.

**Flying boat**
Aircraft with a boat-shaped lower fuselage, allowing it to take off and set down on water. A seaplane has floats to do the same job.

**Metal construction**
Familiar to anyone who flies in a modern aircraft, it was just being perfected in the 1920s and 1930s. Some modern aircraft such as the Voyager, have a composite construction. This uses a paper honeycomb with carbon-fiber stiffener, glued together as a sandwich. Pilots such as Dick Rutan think that composite construction is better than metal.

**Navigator**
Member of aircrew who works out the plane's correct course.

**Oxygen equipment**
Oxygen, the gas we all need to breathe, is compressed into a metal bottle. The oxygen is later piped out from the bottle, then breathed in using a close-fitting face mask.

**Retractable undercarriage**
Wheels which fold up out of the airflow after takeoff.

**Schneider Trophy**
Prize awarded to the winner of the international air races held from 1913 until 1931. Races were held in places as far apart as Monaco, the United States, Italy and Britain.

**Sextant**
Used by navigators to get a "fix" on the sun by day or the stars by night. Knowing the position of Sun or Pole Star a skilled navigator can work out the position of the aircraft.

**Snow plume**
A "tail" of ice particles blown from the side of many high mountains. Mount Everest has a permanent plume blowing from its summit.

**Tailwind**
A following wind which helps an aircraft fly a little faster. A headwind is the reverse and slows an aircraft down. Slow-flying planes can make little headway against a strong headwind.

**Throttle**
The accelerator of an aircraft, used to increase or decrease engine power.

**Torque**
Force produced by any rotating mass, such as an engine and propeller. Tends to twist things in the same direction. Schneider Trophy racers often had takeoff problems caused by their powerful engines. Today's helicopters have a tail rotor to keep them from spinning around under the main rotor. Torque is pronounced "TORK."

**Waterspout**
Curious weather effect, sometimes seen in the tropics. A narrow column of spinning water is sucked up from the water, into the air. You can sometimes see a similar effect on dusty ground on windy days, when "dust devils" – small twisty columns of spinning dust – are sucked up by the wind.

**Weather radar**
Equipment carried on most airliners today. It sends out a radio beam ahead of the plane. Echoes bounce back from solid objects such as other planes or semi-solid clouds are "painted" onto a small TV screen in the cockpit. Radar was not perfected until World War II. Until then aircraft had to fly through or around bad weather. Most aircraft didn't have the performance to fly high like today's aircraft, so they had to fly through the stormy lower atmosphere.

# Index